His

The History of the Monuments, Fine Arts and Archives Program

(Also Known as Monument Men)

By Howard Brinkley

BookCaps™ Study Guides
www.bookcaps.com

© 2013. All Rights Reserved.

Table of Contents

ABOUT HISTORYCAPS 3

INTRODUCTION 4

CHAPTER 1: THE FUHRER MUSEUM 6

CHAPTER 2: THE MONUMENTS, FINE ARTS, AND ARCHIVES COMMISSION 12

   GEORGE STOUT AND THE BIRTH OF THE MONUMENTS MEN . 15
   BOMBING MONTE CASSINO 18

CHAPTER 3: THE MONUMENTS MEN IN FRANCE 22

   JAMES RORIMER 24
   THE LOUVRE 25
   ROSE VALLAND 28
   THE ART TRAIN 31

CHAPTER 4: THE MONUMENTS MEN IN GERMANY 35

   NEUSCHWANSTEIN CASTLE, GERMANY 36
   HARRY ETTLINGER 38

CHAPTER 5: RETURNING THE ART 42

   THE GHENT ALTARPIECE 44
   COLLECTION POINTS 50

CONCLUSION 54

REFERENCES 56

About HistoryCaps

HistoryCaps is an imprint of BookCaps™ Study Guides. With each book, a brief period of history is recapped. We publish a wide array of topics (from baseball and music to science and philosophy), so check our growing catalogue regularly (**www.bookcaps.com**) to see our newest books.

Introduction

The Holocaust was the systematic murder of six million European Jews by Adolf Hitler's Nazi Party. The horrors of the Holocaust have been documented many times. Even those that were not killed, mutilated, or starved in concentration camps were stripped of their citizenship and their identities. The Nazis did not stop there, though. Hitler, in his quest to build an empire, planned and executed the most extensive theft of art and cultural treasures in history.

A group of art historians, museum curators, scholars, and others with an expertise in art accepted the enormous responsibility of traveling to the front lines of World War II in an effort to protect art before it could be stolen or recover the art that fell into the hands of the Nazis. Even more lent their expertise when the fighting ended, remaining in Europe for years after the war was over. They were called "Venus fixers" by the troops but have since come to be known as the Monuments Men.

Acting on orders from General Dwight D. Eisenhower, who had the backing of President Franklin D. Roosevelt, many of the Monuments Men – and women – put their lives on the line for art. By doing so, they preserved not just paintings, sculptures, and tapestries, but a significant portion of the culture that makes life worth living. As Mikhail Piotrovsky, the director of the State Hermitage Museum in Russia, said, "Art belongs to humanity. Art is what makes us human."

Chapter 1: The Fuhrer Museum

At the age of 18, an aspiring art student moved from Linz, Austria to Vienna. It was 1905, and he made his living in typical bohemian fashion by earning a few cents here and there selling drawings that he copied from postcards. On at least one occasion, he lived in a hostel for the homeless. His real dream was to attend the renowned Vienna Fine Arts Academy. He applied twice and was rejected both times.

Adolf Hitler was convinced that it was a panel of Jewish art instructors who denied his application. Historians like to speculate on how the experience impacted him. Was it the rejection to art school that shaped him into the ruthless man that he became? What if he had been accepted and had gone on to be an artist? The world will never know, but what is known is that Hitler's passion for art never left him. As he ascended to become the dictator of Germany as a representative of the National Socialist German Worker's Party, known as the Nazis, Hitler had a new dream.

In the years leading up to World War II, Hitler had already begun to prepare to create not just the world's finest museum, but to transform his adopted hometown of Linz into the cultural capital of the world. Members of the Nazi Secret Service, led by Heinrich Himmler, traveled throughout Europe and created an inventory listing every piece of famous art along with its value and its location. Hitler had already started collecting pieces for his own private collection, but his museum in Linz was going to be much more. Hitler wanted Linz to rival Florence, Italy.

It was in Italy that his plan took shape. In May 1938, Hitler made his second trip there. He had been to Italy once before when he visited Italian dictator Benito Mussolini in Venice in 1934. On his second trip, he saw Rome. The sheer history and wonder of the ruins of the magnificent Roman Empire left Hitler in awe. He was already discussing plans with Albert Speer, his personal architect, to rebuild Berlin. After seeing Rome, Hitler told Speer to recreate Berlin so that future generations would feel the same awe that Rome inspired.

Hitler was equally taken with Florence, and he kept Mussolini waiting for hours as he methodically made his way through the famed Uffizi Gallery. All Mussolini could see was room after room of paintings but for Hitler, he saw the past and the future all rolled up into one package. That would be in Linz, where he was viewed as a hero to his country and his race. By 1938, Hitler had already stripped German Jews of their citizenship and nearly all of their possessions. The Secret Service looted their private art collections, their silver and even took their family photos. For this, many in Linz loved Hitler.

If Hitler was going to build an empire, he decided that his empire needed an artistic center. Linz was not going to be just the home of a great museum. It would be the home of the Fuhrer Museum. He was the Fuhrer. He had given himself this title to proclaim his ultimate authority over Germany. The Fuhrer Museum would be nothing less than the best art museum in the world in a setting befitting his ultimate artistic legacy.

Hitler's agents scoured Europe as his power grew and they simply took what they wanted. They tried to give the illusion that it was all obtained legally. Jews who fled Europe due to the Holocaust had their citizenship revoked and, therefore, the possessions they left behind were "ownerless." From museums, the Nazis took art, tapestries, and other notable works of art and kept it all hidden for the sake of "protecting" it. One of the leaders of this operation was Alfred Rosenberg who headed up a special task force called the Einsatzstab Reichsleiter Rosenberg (ERR). Between 1940 and 1944, Rosenberg robbed Jewish art collectors and dealers in France of Belgium of their artwork and sent them to the Jeu de Paume, a museum situated between the Louvre and the Tuileries Gardens in Paris. While housed at the Jeu de Paume, the art was processed by "Special Staff for Pictorial Art" and then shipped to Germany. Over 20,000 stolen works of art were photographed and catalogued at the museum before transported to German storage facilities, awaiting their grand unveiling at the Fuhrer Museum.

Hitler took it upon himself to draw up plans for a massive, sprawling complex in Linz that included an opera house, libraries, a theater, and a mausoleum for his tomb. The industrial Danube riverfront of Linz was to be rebuilt into a carefully planned district with wide pedestrian walkways, parade grounds, parks, and cafes. It was the ultimate vindication for the rejected art school student. Hitler liked to gaze at the model of his new Linz, which eventually grew to take up the better part of an entire room. When he holed up in his underground bunker in Berlin in 1945 to hide from the advancing Allied troops, he took part of the model. He wanted it to be one of the last things he saw and most likely it was since it was in the Fuhrer Bunker that Hitler and his wife, Eva Braun, committed suicide. However, in his will, Hitler said that the Fuhrer Museum should still be built.

Every Christmas, Hitler received green leather-bound albums containing copies of superb paintings that would one day fill the Fuhrer Museum walls. There were 31 albums in all. One of those albums ended up on the shelf of an American G.I. from Ohio. John Pistone, who served with General George Patton's Third Army, took the 13th album from Hitler's home in the Bavarian Alps in 1945 as a war souvenir. Like many soldiers, he wanted proof that he had been to Berghof. Pistone did not realize what he had nor was he particularly interested in finding out. It was not until 2009, when a contractor who was installing Pistone's new washer and dryer noticed the album, that the story behind the album came to light.

The contractor did some internet research, contacted Robert Edsel, the president of the Monuments Men Foundation, and it was Edsel who persuaded Pistone to return the album to Germany. It took time for Pistone to agree, though. He had kept the album for so long that he was reluctant to give it up but after reading Edsel's book about the Monuments Men, Pistone realized that the album was important beyond being just a war souvenir. In a ceremony at the State Department in Washington, D.C. in 2010, Pistone personally gave Hitler's album to a German ambassador.

Chapter 2: The Monuments, Fine Arts, and Archives Commission

As German troops rolled through western Europe in the beginning of World War II, it became apparent that Allied forces could only liberate Europe by occupying it. Fighting the Nazi hold on Europe would require massive amounts of armed troops and bombing raids, beginning in Italy and France. The site of the biggest war the world had ever seen was also the site of some of the world's most treasured artistic and cultural symbols, all of which were in danger of destruction.

President Franklin D. Roosevelt was an art lover and did not want to destroy irreplaceable pieces of European culture in the process of winning a war. With that in mind, he authorized the "American Commission for the Protection and Salvage of Artistic and Historic Monuments in War Areas" on June 23, 1943. It is more commonly known as the Roberts Commission, named for its chairman, Supreme Court Justice Owen Roberts. From that commission sprung the Monuments, Fine Arts and Archives commission (MFAA). The MFAA was eventually staffed with 345 soldiers who worked with military commanders, soldiers, and various civilians to protect Europe's cultural heritage. The majority of the people assigned to the MFAA went to Europe after the fighting ended. A select few were on the front lines with the troops. This corps of officers was made up of museum curators, art historians, architects, and art restorers who could lend expertise to the operation.

General Dwight D. Eisenhower issued his first monument protection order six months after the Allied campaign in North Africa. While there, Allied soldiers helped themselves to books, art, and other treasures to take home as war souvenirs. Some even took stuffed monkeys from the national zoo. The lack of respect shown to the country's culture was giving the Allies a bad reputation and Eisenhower worried about the impression his troops were making.

On December 29, 1943, Eisenhower said from Italy of the country's great monuments, "We are bound to respect those monuments so far as war allows." He repeated his orders before the landing on Omaha Beach on D-Day. Eisenhower's order said that it was "the responsibility of every commander to protect and respect" any monument, building, or similar cultural work or area unless it became a "military necessity" to destroy them. If it was a matter of preserving lives or a building then the building would have to go, but all care had to be taken to prevent such destruction, if possible. For the first time, an army fought a war with an eye toward protecting history.

Before Allied forces invaded Italy, MFAA officers made a list of important cultural sites that were near battle locations and gave the list to military commanders. When battles were over, and an area was secured by the Allies, the Monuments Men went into that area to assess any damage to cultural sites. Deane Keller recalled that the people of Florence were traumatized by the bombing of their city, and it took some effort to build their trust so that he could enlist the help of local civilians to help prevent further damage, particularly from looters. When Keller escorted trucks full of Florence's stolen art back home after the war ended, the citizens of Florence wept and cheered at its return.

It was important that there were MFAA officers on the front lines as the fighting or occurred or immediately after the fighting ended to make sure that Eisenhower's protection orders were followed. It was also important that the Monuments Men be made officers if there was any chance of military commanders following the plans. Still, the Monuments Men were only advisors and had it not been for the involvement of Justice Owens, it is possible that the army may have resisted having Monuments Men at the front lines. Once they were there, it was up to the MFAA officers to be diligent in their duties, an enormous task made all the more difficult by the fact that there was no process or precedent for what they were trying to do.

George Stout and the Birth of the Monuments Men

After the fall of Paris to the Nazis in June 1940 and before FDR created the commission that became the MFAA, a group of Harvard faculty and local residents created a group to help provide guidance on the preservation of European art and other expertise on European culture. The leader of that group was the associate director of the Fogg Art Museum at Harvard, Paul Sachs, who created a course called "Museum Work and Museum Problems" for future museum curators and directors. As a member of the Roberts Commission, Sachs created maps and guidebooks for use in identifying art and monuments in Europe. He was also responsible for recruiting several of the MFAA officers.

When war broke out in Europe, Sachs and George Stout, an art conservator at Fogg, created a slideshow for the directors of the top art museums in the United States. As they all gathered at the Metropolitan Museum of Art in New York, Sachs and Stout reminded the museum directors of what war can do. They showed slides of an empty National Gallery in London, its art moved to Manod Quarry for protection; London's Tate Gallery littered with broken pieces of glass; an empty Louvre in Paris; paintings at Rijksmuseum in Amsterdam stacked on the floor, waiting their next move. Sach and Fogg made their point, and while American museum directors vowed to keep museums open as long as possible, many works in the care of American museums were also hidden until the end of the war.

Stout was active in educating museum directors on museum safety. He discussed the proper way to pack paintings, how to avoid heat damage, and the damage that bombs could do to museum windows. Bombs were a new part of modern warfare, and it was the bombs that most concerned art curators. Stout also began to push for a coordinated effort to protect and preserve the cultural symbols of the war-torn areas of Europe. Stout wrote a pamphlet in the summer of 1942 and said that it was the responsibility of the nations fighting the war to protect the art, churches, and monuments not just as a means of preserving culture, but to show respect. Stout wrote that "these things belong not only to a particular people but also to the heritage of mankind."

Stout's plan to have a conservation corps of officers went nowhere for a while. By January 1, 1943, Stout gave up on the idea and moved from reservist to active duty in the U.S. Navy. At least by actively serving in the war, he felt like he was contributing to the war effort rather than treading water with a conservation plan that could not seem to stick. However, while he worked for the Navy testing camouflage paint for airplanes, Colonel James Shoemaker had become interested in Stout's plan. Shoemaker, the head of the U.S. Military Government Division, contacted Stout and asked for more information. When Sachs wrote to Stout to tell him about FDR's commission in September 1943, Stout was underwhelmed. To Stout, a commission seemed like another layer of bureaucracy, and it was far short of the conservation corps that he had envisioned.

Bombing Monte Cassino

Britain. As Stout had predicted, the MFAA was wrapped in bureaucratic layers, and while there were Monuments Men in Italy in 1944, there were none at Monte Cassino until it was too late. Located approximately halfway between Naples and Rome, Monte Cassino was the first test of the edict from the Joint Chiefs of Staff that cultural monuments and artifacts be preserved. In the fall of 1943, word had already gone out that the abbey at Monte Cassino had to be saved from harm, if at all possible. The abbey sits on the top of mountain, overlooking the town of Cassino. It was founded in 529 A.D. by Saint Benedictine and has been considered a national monument since 1866.

When U.S. troops arrived on the mainland of Italy in September 1943, Germans welcomed them by declaring over a loudspeaker that they had the Americans surrounded. They launched a bloody battle that so decimated the Allied troops that an American unit and a British unit had to be combined. The mountainous regions of Italy can be cold and damp. Soldiers fighting at Monte Cassino learned that first hand as the slogged their way through mud and later, snow, as they battled the German troops on the mountain. Germans were stationed all across the mountain, and Allied troops took gunfire as they tried to trudge their way to the top. Stories filtered home about American soldiers dying at Monte Cassino. Looming above them all was the abbey. Inside were monks and residents of the town who were convinced that the Allies would never bomb the abbey because it was a national treasure. Approximately 2,000 people had taken refuge inside the stone walls.

However, with Hitler's Germany army seemingly everywhere that fall, some Allied commanders became convinced that Nazis were in the abbey. For the Allied infantry, it was a frustrating situation to be given the order of taking the mountain but yet also being told to not harm the building at the top. What if the Nazis were in there? Major General Howard Kippenberger from New Zealand said even if they were not in there, it was only a matter of time before Nazis overtook the abbey. Some of the French and American commanders objected to attacking it, but many of the soldiers, British commanders, and citizens on the home front wanted the abbey destroyed. Families of soldiers did not want their sons, brothers, and husbands to die while protecting a building. Kippenberger finally said that he could not ask soldiers to storm the mountain if there was building on it that could be housing the enemy.

The ancient abbey was bombed on February 15, 1944. Soldiers and war correspondents on the scene cheered as the walls of the abbey crumbled. U.S. Army Air Forces General Ira C. Eaker said it was an example of the Allied strength. Germany and Italy said that the Allies were barbaric if they were willing to destroy such a structure merely on the possibility that it was occupied. The Nazis were, in fact, not in the abbey. They had respected its cultural significance and were in the valley below it. However, when the Allies bombed the abbey, they opened the door for Nazi paratroopers to drop into the ruins and strengthen the defensive position of the troops already on the ground. When the dust cleared, a Nazi flag could be seen flying in the debris.

The Allies eventually took Monte Cassino, but it took three months to do it. The number of wounded or killed reached 54,000. Major Ernest DeWald was the first of the Monuments Men to arrive in Cassino on May 27, 1944, one week after the Allied victory. DeWald was an art professor at Princeton University and the director of the MFAA in Italy from 1943 until 1946. He surveyed the damage of the abbey and found that the church was utterly destroyed. The library, art galleries, and monastery were gone. The bronze doors and mosaic tile dating back to the 11th century had been reduced to rubble.

Chapter 3: The Monuments Men in France

Following the catastrophe in Italy, the Civil Affairs branch of AMGOT – the Allied Military Government for Occupied Territories – was determined to get more trained MFAA officers ready for the invasion of France. One of the first officers that Paul Sachs picked was George Stout, who arrived in England in March 1944. It was just a month after the bombing of Monte Cassino. The MFAA had moved into the American School in Shrivenham and was using it as a training center.

In the earliest days of the operation, it was in desperate need of structure. There was no official mission statement, no chain of command, and no appointed leader. They were given no transportation, no manual, and there was not even anyone responsible for coordinating military resources such as getting uniforms and rations. Most of the Monuments Men had no formal training. When their orders were processed, they simply showed up to their new unit. With no chain of command, the Monuments Men had to create a process as they went along, starting with passing out lists of protected European monuments. Other than a basic understanding that once in the field they should record the condition of monuments when the battles were over, supervise any immediate repair work, and making sure that monuments or sites did not sustain any more damage, they did not have a specific assignment.

Without an official commander, Stout served as the ad hoc leader. He had written to Sachs and given his recommendations for the Roberts Commission, which included 16 people to serve as staff for each MFAA officer. However, Stout realized that finding that many people to serve on the fronts lines when he knew of only a dozen people in total who were qualified to do the work was probably impossible.

James Rorimer

James Rorimer was the curator of the medieval art collection at the Cloisters at the Metropolitan Museum of Art when he was drafted into the army in 1943. He had a rather meteoric rise through the ranks of the Met, achieving the title of curator only seven years after graduating from Harvard. The ambitious and energetic infantry private was recommended for the MFAA by Sachs and was sent to England in 1944 shortly after Stout arrived. He was promoted to captain and while in Shrivenham, Rorimer took German classes six days a week to complement his fluency in French.

A testament to Rorimer's resolve came in Normandy at the chateau of Comte de Germigny. The house, which was on the protected monuments list, was badly burned by Allied bombs. When Rorimer went to the house, he saw most of the walls laying crumbled on the ground and a bulldozer getting ready to knock down the remaining ones. Rorimer told the driver to stop and advised him that, as a historic home, it was not supposed to be destroyed. When the commanding officer came on the scene, Rorimer told him, too, that the house was not supposed to be destroyed. The commander seemed uninterested in the order as well as in Rorimer and walked away. However, Rorimer persisted and told him that he had taken a photo of the wall for his report. After a brief staredown, the commander relented, and the home was saved from demolition.

After weeks of inspecting monuments in Normandy, Rorimer arrived in newly liberated Paris in August 1944, four years after the Nazi occupation of the French capital began. One of the first things he did was save the famed Jardin des Tuileries, not from the Germans but from the Allies. The garden is situated between the Louvre and the Place de Concord. It is as much a symbol of Paris as Central Park is of New York City. Before the Allied and French Resistance forces pushed the Nazis out of the city, the Nazis had dug trenches ringed with barbed wire throughout the park. When Rorimer learned that the Allies were going to use the park for an encampment, he protested. He could not accept the thought of latrines being built in the Tuileries, and even though it took a series of meetings to make his point, Rorimer got the Army to change its mind.

The Louvre

Before the Nazis ever arrived – actually, before most Parisians could even conceive of the idea of Germans occupying their city – Jacques Jaujard began evacuating the Louvre. Jaujard was the director of French National Museums. The massive museum complex, first established in 1783, is home to some of the world's most cherished works of art including the *Mona Lisa* and the *Venus de Milo*. When American troops initially arrived in Paris, they used the courtyard outside of the entrance to the Louvre as a temporary prison camp for German prisoners of war. Inside the museum, though, were miles of walls, empty except for handwritten notes about what used to hang there.

Jaujard supervised the removal of the art. It was not the first time he had done something like that. During the Spanish Civil War, he helped remove art from the Prado in Madrid. When he became director of French National Museums in 1939, he immediately made plans to protect the Louvre's art from damage from the war. The *Mona Lisa* was whisked away in its own climate-controlled truck after being transported out of the museum on an ambulance stretcher. The *Mona Lisa* made it to is destination just fine, but the curator that rode in the back of the truck with the masterpiece was nearly unconscious from a lack of air. The famous Leonardo da Vinci painting moved at least six times during the course of the war.

Visitors to the Louvre are likely familiar with the massive Greek statue called *Winged Victory of Samothrace* that is at the top of the museum's main staircase. That, too, was removed. Workers were able to move it using a pulley and wooden ramp system. From there they loaded it into a truck, where it spent the war at Chateau de Valencay, along with the *Venus de Milo* and Michelangelo's *Slaves*. These pieces, like most of the others, were sent to castles and chateaus to keep them out of the main line of fire of bombs. Workers at one of the country villas went so far as to write "Musee de Louvre" on the lawn so that pilots would known that protected pieces of art were inside. At first, Jaujard did not know that the art needed to be protected from Hitler's men because they wanted to steal it, not destroy it.

The Nazis took over Paris on June 14, 1940. Two weeks later, Hitler ordered members of his staff to watch over the works in the French National Collection, as well as some artwork and documents from private collections of Jews. He intended to use them as part of his peace negotiations when the time came and then he was going to use the peace treaty to take possession of France's prized cultural symbols. Within days of the Nazi occupation, Otto Abetz, the Nazi ambassador to Paris, said that the Nazis would take custody of the art that had not already been hidden. Abetz then ordered the art from 15 of Paris's top art dealers confiscated. The majority of those art dealers were Jewish.

Rose Valland

In the fall of 1940, Hitler told Reich Leader Alfred Rosenberg's Special Task Force (ERR) to search through unoccupied western territories for anything that might prove to be valuable to Germany. It was through the ERR that the Nazis processed some of France's most valued artwork and other cultural symbols, almost all stolen from private collectors. The Jeu de Paume, next door to the Louvre, became the headquarters for the Nazi art theft operation.

Throughout the four years that the Nazis used the Jeu de Paume as its warehouse and clearinghouse of French art, they had no idea that they were being watched by an unassuming French woman. They also did not know that she happened to be fluent in German. In the beginning of the occupation, the Nazis tried to make a show of how reasonable they could be and told the woman that she could stay on her job at the Jeu de Paume. The Gestapo guards that stood over the intake, cataloging, and outflow of art did not realize, though, that Rose Valland was a spy, and she was watching every move they made. She was nearly caught a couple of times. Once, she was seen trying to decipher an address and the Nazi officer that caught her told her she should be shot. Valland did not back down, though, and believed that showing strength was the only way to survive the Nazi occupation.

Overall, though, the ERR saw Valland as the woman who watered the plants and took care of minor building maintenance. In reality, she was a curator at the Louvre and a member of the French Resistance who had been asked to work at the Jeu de Paume by Jacques Jaujard. Valland watched the ERR by day and unloaded her remarkable memory every night into her carefully detailed journal. As time went on, she got bold enough to take notes because the information was getting to be too hard to remember. That progressed to taking the ERR files home at night. She recorded it all. She recorded the names of people who came and went, the art that came in and where it came from, and then where the art was going once on the trains out of Paris and into Germany. The Nazis were well known as thorough and meticulous with their own cataloging, and they took photos of their stolen goods. Each night, Valland smuggled the negatives out of the museum, made her own copies, and then returned the negatives before anyone noticed. It did occur to her as she wrestled with insomnia and the sheer terror of what might happen if she was ever caught that she might not live to see the end of the Nazi occupation.

Valland provided Jaujard and with valuable information in their weekly meetings. He then passed on that information on. A great deal of Valland's information came from Dr. Walter Borchers, who was the art historian responsible for cataloging the stolen art. He often confided in Valland and much of what he told her made its way to the French Resistance. Still, not all of the ERR trusted her and more than once she was banned from the museum after being accused of being a spy. Some of the accusations may have been Nazi intimidation tactics. However, she always denied it, and they always let her back because it was convenient to use her as an excuse for when things went wrong. Valland also happened to know that one of the ERR, Bruno Lohse, was stealing some of the art from himself. Lohse knew that she was aware of his activities and apparently did not want to risk giving her a reason to tell.

As it became clear that the Allied troops would soon be in Paris, and the Nazis were wrapping up their art stealing business, Valland sensed that she was soon going to be dispensable. She was not going to be of any value to them and, in fact, she was a witness to the all that had gone on at the Jeu de Paume. Valland realized that she was not above being eliminated if it made sense for them to do it. She was especially wary of Colonel Kurt von Behr, who had been so joyous when he arrived four years ago but with defeat staring him in the face seemed angry. During the final days of the occupation, Valland resisted the temptation to push von Behr, who seemed on the verge of a mental breakdown.

The Art Train

With the Allies on the way, Valland watched as the Nazi soldiers carelessly crammed paintings into crates without even bothering to properly pack them. She had learned that the last trucks of art were going to the Aubervilliers train station outside of Paris and from there the crates were to be unloaded onto railroad cars. Valland thought that this was a stroke of luck because it would be nearly impossible to trace trucks. Trains were a different matter.

On August 2, 1944, nearly 150 crates of art stolen from French collectors were loaded into rail cars. They sat their for a few days as the Nazis waited for another shipment from a separate looting operation. Von Behr grew more frustrated the longer the trains sat motionless in Aubervilliers. Valland knew this, as well as what was in the crates and where they were headed. She suggested to Jaujard that perhaps he might see what he could do to delay the train's departure even more.

Jaujard gave the information to his contacts in the French Resistance. When the art train was finally ready to depart on August 10, it could not leave because the French railroad workers had gone on strike. The tracks were open again two days later, but the art train was moved aside to a side track as a train full of Germans and their personal possessions came through the station, taking the scared Germans back home. By this point, the Nazis who were guarding the art train had been at it for 10 days and rumors spread that the French army was en route. The train finally left after a three-week delay, but made it only as far as Le Bourget, just a few miles down the track. The Germans were told that the train was so heavy that the weight was causing mechanical problems. This resulted in another 48-hour delay, which was just enough time for the French Resistance to derail two other trains down the line, effectively preventing the art train from every leaving Paris. Unfortunately, a two-month delay in acting on the information provided by Valland allowed some of the crates to be opened and looted. Thirty-six of the crates, which contained work by masters such as Renoir, Degas, Picasso, and Gauguin, were eventually sent to the Louvre, but Valland was frustrated by the delay. She was also bitter when an article in *Le Figaro* gave credit to the French railway system for the recovery of the art.

Three months after Rorimer had arrived in Paris, his friend Jaujard told him of the spy amongst the ERR. When Jaujard told him who it was, Rorimer struggled to remember her. It was her rather plain appearance that served her so well. She was, in many regards, forgettable. Jaujard wanted Rorimer to talk to her, but Rorimer was not convinced that she knew anything useful. He was also suspicious of the fact that Valland had not already rushed to tell him what she knew.

Jaujard explained that Valland had shared information with him, but that many in France were wary of collaborators. It was hard to know who to trust. On the day that Paris was liberated, Valland was threatened by her countrymen and accused of being a collaborator with the Nazis. They accused of her of harboring Nazis in the Louvre. She was intent on not allowing anyone into the basement of the Louvre, where the museum's art collection was stored. However, at gunpoint, Valland led a group of Frenchmen into the basement to prove that the only thing there was art, not a group of Nazis.

Jaujard also explained to Rorimer that the French government was overwhelmed with trying to function again after removing the Nazi occupiers. Even though the government was given information from Valland, they were slow to act on it. In one instance when Valland had informed Jaujard of 112 cases of stolen art, it took two months to retrieve it. By that time, much of it had been picked through and would likely never be recovered. That is why they wanted Rorimer to get involved. They believed that the only way to get anything done was for someone not affiliated with the French government to do it.

It did take some time for Valland to trust Rorimer. Jaujard pushed her toward partnering with him, but she was not sure that she could simply hand over all of the intelligence that she had obtained over the four-year occupation and put it in the hands of an American officer. Through it all, from the first days of the occupation to the days when the Germans arrived at the Jardin des Tuileries to fight off the French resistance, Valland had risked her life for the art. She had to be sure of Rorimer before she gave him what she knew. Even when she was sure of him, she told him that she could not tell him what she knew unless he was on the front lines in Germany. That is where the art was, and the information would only be of use to him if he was there. Rorimer applied for a transfer within days of their conversation.

Chapter 4: The Monuments Men in Germany

On March 1, 1945, James Rorimer learned that he would be the MFAA officer for the Seventh Army. Not long after that, Rose Valland invited him to visit her at her apartment. She knew of his appointment to the Seventh Army, and, after several months of giving him bits and pieces of information, she finally Rorimer what he wanted to know. Valland had been the steward of the information about some of the greatest artistic treasures in the world, and now she trusted Rorimer with that information on to Rorimer. She was quite sure of her facts. The only question was whether or not the Nazis had been vindictive in the face of defeat and destroyed the stolen art.

At the meeting at her apartment, Valland showed Rorimer photos of important people from the ERR. Hermann Goering, Bruno Lohse, and Kurt von Behr, to name a few. The photos showed the men inspecting paintings or working at their desks. Other photos were of the artwork themselves, hanging frameless on walls. These photos were taken using the negatives that she smuggled out of the Jeu de Paume. Along with the photos, Valland produced a treasure trove of her own: copies of train manifestos, receipts, and other documents to confirm which pieces of art had been processed through the Jeu de Paume.

Neuschwanstein Castle, Germany

Rose Valland also shared with Rorimer the names of various art repositories used by the Nazis, including Buxheim, Hohenschwangau, and Heilbronn. All of these locations were in Rorimer's new territory within the Seventh Army. However, the biggest one was at a location familiar to many people. The Neuschwanstein Castle in Germany is known to Disney fans as the model for the Sleeping Beauty castle. It was built by King Ludwig II, known as "Mad Ludwig," as his private refuge high in the Bavarian Alps. It is as remote as it was beautiful and Valland told Rorimer that it was were thousands of works of art stolen from France were being stored.

When the Allied forces took a town not far from Neuschwanstein months later, Rorimer had his chance. The Germans had left the castle unguarded so that when the American soldiers arrived, they had no trouble gaining entry. The soldiers were aware of its importance and had made sure that nobody, regardless of rank, entered any of the rooms. Interestingly, the Nazis kept the castle's staff rather than replace them with their own, so when Rorimer, his assistant, John Skilton, and a group of guards entered the castle they were led by the Neuschwanstein custodian. They made their way through a maze of incredibly steep stairs, designed by a theater stage designer and not an architect. At the top of the stairwells were locked wooden doors that required enormous keys that were almost comical in size. Some stairs led to rooms of odd shapes and sizes; some led to balconies with soaring views.

Every room was filled boxes and crates, some of which were never touched. The initials ERR had been stenciled over the French symbols of art collectors. Racks and platforms held more boxes of paintings. Some paintings were simply jammed onto shelves; some rooms held nothing but gold pieces of art or décor. In other rooms, they found furniture while others held household goods or tapestries. Books and engravings were packed into other rooms. Locked in a room secured by a steel door was the jewelry collection belonging to Maurice de Rothschild, the Senator of France, and over a thousand pieces of silver that belonged to investment banker Pierre David-Weill.

Needless to say, Rorimer was shocked and overwhelmed by what he had discovered. He was also grateful that the ERR had taken the time to catalog every item they had stolen and shipped to Neuschwanstein. There were over 6,000 pieces in the castle alone, not to mention the 15,000 other pieces that had gone to other repositories. Without it, it would have taken years, if not decades, to determine what was there. It took the Seventh Army over six weeks to evacuate the art from the castle, most of which had to be carried by hand down the castle's steep and winding stairs.

Harry Ettlinger

Unlike most of the people associated with the MFAA, Private Harry Ettlinger was not a curator or art historian. He was a G.I. from New Jersey who also happened to be a Jew born in Karlsruhe, Germany. He and his family escaped to America in 1938, and it took the war to take Ettlinger back to Germany. It did not go unnoticed that he spoke German fluently. He had been pulled off the front lines at the Battle of the Bulge to serve as an interpreter at the Nuremberg trials, which would hear the cases of Nazi officials charged with war crimes. Hitler escaped his trial by committing suicide.

However, Ettlinger ended up with the MFAA instead, working with James Rorimer. For the youthful Ettlinger, the slow pace of what, for him, had been a rather dull war suddenly picked up. Among his first tasks in his new assignment in May 1945 was to interpret for Rorimer in his interview with Heinrich Hoffman, Hitler's friend and photographer. Rorimer had already spent several days working on Hoffman, who predictably said that he was only following Hitler's orders and that he only purchased painting from reputable dealers,

After that, Ettlinger went with Rorimer to Berchtesgaden in the German Bavarian Alps, not far from Hitler's mountainous retreat. There they found the vast collection of Hermann Goering, the commander-in-chief of the Luftwaffe, the German Air Force. Not all of the loot plundered from Europe ended up in storage, awaiting its display at the Furhrer Museum. Goering diverted hundreds of pieces of art for his own private collection.

Rorimer also took Ettlinger on his first trip to Neuschwanstein. After weeks of translating documents and numbers, seeing the rooms packed with stolen property brought Ettlinger's understanding of the war and what the Nazis inflicted on the Jews to a whole new level. Ettlinger said years later, "My knowledge of the Holocaust started really with the realization that it was not only the taking of lives…but the taking of all of their belongings."

It was at the Heilbronn salt mine that Ettlinger fully grasped the enormity of what the MFAA was trying to do. Thousands of pieces of art were stored in mines, which were just the right temperature for preserving art. Had it not been for Rorimer, there may have been nothing left to preserve. When he arrived, there it was just after a 10-day battle had ended and there was no electricity. This resulted in a failure in the mine's pumping system, which left the mines in danger of flooding. Fortunately, Eisenhower responded to Rorimer's request for Army engineers to go the scene to restore the pumps and save the art.

Dale Ford, an interior designer and a lieutenant assigned to the MFAA, worked with three Germans to try and determine just what was in the Heilbronn mine. Ettlinger's job was to descend into the dark mine, hundreds of feet below the surface, with two German miners as his guides, and bring the art back up above ground. The Heilbronn mine was comprised of miles of chambers and within those chambers were 40,000 cases of art.

Ettlinger worked from the carefully created lists left behind by the ERR. This did help him match up art, their crate numbers, and their corresponding locations on the shelves. However, it was cold and dark in the mines, and the paths veered off in many different direction. It was easy to get lost. Ettlinger also had to be aware that any of the crates could be booby-trapped. A particularly frightening discovery was a room sealed off by bricks. When the wall was torn down, he discovered tables full of bottles of nitroglycerin, which had separated over time. Had he not discovered the bottles in time to permit the experts to get down there and retrieve them, the bottles would have exploded about a month later. Most likely, that was the intent of whoever built the wall.

Chapter 5: Returning the Art

Harry Ettlinger spent nearly a year helping retrieve art from the mines at Heilbronn and at Kochendorf. Not all of it was stolen. Some of it legally belonged to Germany, and the Allies determined that it must be returned to its proper owners, along with all of the art that was recovered. General Eisenhower said that it was important for the relationship with their Allies that the stolen items are given back to the country that lost it. In the summer of 1945, he ordered that the most important pieces be shipped back immediately and said they would work on a system to return the rest.

Simply sifting through all that Goering had stolen was a challenge. Goering lived the highlife during the Nazi occupation of Paris. He indulged in lavish dinners, parties, champagne, and, of course, art. He did have a good eye and knew which pieces Hitler would want for his museum in Linz. However, he visited the Jeu de Paume 20 times and took over 700 works of art for himself. He had them shipped by railroad to his country estate outside of Berlin. Already an art collector, Goering soon needed to add massive galleries onto his home to display it all. When his collection was discovered, he had accumulated an astounding 1,700 paintings.

Several of the pieces in Goering's collection came from the gallery of a Jewish art dealer from France named Andre Seligmann. He and his family fled France and settled in New York, where Seligmann opened another gallery in November 1941. One of the paintings that was stolen from Seligmann by the Nazis was *The Young Lovers* by Francois Boucher, dating back to the 1700s. The Boucher painting wound up with Goering but was not among those returned to the Seligmann family. In about 2003, a researcher for the National Gallery of Art in New York was researching a book on the Goering collection, and while doing internet research on *The Young Lovers*, she discovered that it was in the possession of the Utah Museum of Fine Arts.

The researcher called the museum and the museum staff confirmed that they did, indeed, have the stolen Boucher painting. Museum staffers did not realize that it was stolen art. It had been donated to them from someone who bought it from a gallery in New York in 1972. How it got to New York in the first place is not known. The Utah museum director and staff cooperated with getting the painting returned to the Seligmann family. Seligmann's daughter described the experience as "emotional" when she traveled to the museum in 2004 to receive the long lost painting. As for Goering, he was the highest ranked Nazi official to be tried at Nuremberg and was sentenced to death. He committed suicide in his cell before he could be executed.

The Ghent Altarpiece

The most important piece of art in Belgium is the *Adoration of the Mystic Lamb*, more commonly known as the Ghent Altarpiece. It dates back to the early 15th century is made of 12 panels that stand 12 feet high and 16 feet across. Eight of the panels are hinged. The piece was begun by Hubert van Eyck, who died in 1426 before it could be completed. His brother, Jan, finished the piece in 1432. The central panel is a painting of the Lamb of God on an altar. Two of the panels are nude portraits of Adam and Eve. When the intricate piece was unveiled in Ghent at St. Bavo's Cathedral, the Dutch were shocked by the realism. Each detail, including facial expressions, clothing, trees, and jewels was depicted with exceptional care. The piece was not only breathtaking, but it transformed Dutch art.

The Belgian government tried to get the Ghent Altarpiece, along with other noteworthy works of art, out of the country and to the Vatican for its protection in May 1940. The three trucks carrying the Belgian art got only as far as the border of France when Italy declared war on Western Europe. The trucks turned around and took their cargo to a chateau that was also serving as an art repository in Pau, in the southwestern region of France. The drivers could only hope that the art would be safe there.

Of course, Hitler coveted the Ghent Altarpiece. He logically understood that he could not take it without expecting some sort of condemnation, but he believed he was entitled to it. It was part of the "spoils of war." He had similar feelings about the *Mona Lisa* and the Rembrandt painting *The Night Watch*. He even knew where those paintings were, but he left them alone. Hitler could not resist the Ghent Altarpiece, though. Besides, he thought, it actually belongs to Germany. Six of the panels were owned by Germany before World War I. After the Germans signed the Treaty of Versailles, which ended the war and assigned blame for the war on Germany, the panels were given to Belgium as part of war reparations that Germany was forced to repay. Hitler despised the Treaty of Versailles.

Therefore, Hitler came to conclude that taking the Ghent Altarpiece would fix the humiliation of the Treaty of Versailles and return the piece to Germany, where it could take its rightful place in the Fuhrer Museum. In July 1942, Hitler sent a secret delegation to the chateau in Pau. When the French refused to give the Ghent Altarpiece to Hitler's men, the Nazis contacted Pierre Laval, the head of the government in Vichy, France, which was under Nazi control. The superintendent at the chateau was ordered, via telegram, to give the piece to the Nazis.

Robert Posey was the Monuments Man charged with finding the masterpiece. He and fellow MFAA officer Lincoln Kierstein would find it at Altausee, the largest of salt mines and the mine that housed Hitler's personal stash of art. At first, Austrian art was transferred there for safekeeping. Starting in 1944, it was underground in Altausee, Austria that much of Europe's greatest artistic masterpieces waited to be installed at the Fuhrer Museum until, of course, Germany was on the verge of losing the war. At that point, it is likely that the art was destined to be destroyed.

Eight bombs had been placed in the Altausee mine on the order of August Eigruber, a high-ranking Austrian Nazi official, in April 1945. He knew that the Allied troops were getting close to the mine, and he wanted to destroy the art before it could be discovered. It appears that Hitler did not want the art destroyed, and he countermanded the order. After all, he still wanted his museum in Linz built. However, when Hitler committed suicide, Eigruber had the bombs placed, anyway.

Exactly what happened to prevent the ultimate art destruction is not known, but Lincoln Kierstein's explanation is the most accepted one. He said that Austrian miners found the crates with the bombs and secretly removed them from the mine's chambers. They then detonated charges in the mine tunnels, which served to collapse and seal the mine. It took six tons of explosives and 502 timing switches to get the job done This either served to bluff Eigruber into thinking that his order had been carried out, or it simply kept anyone else from getting in there to do any damage.

Posey and Kierstein arrived at Altausee on May 16, 1945. By this point, the village was occupied by a small contingent of American troops. Rumors swirled about how the mine was blown and whether or not the contents were destroyed. Austrian miners, working under the orders of the U.S. military, started clearing the mine so that the Monuments Men could get in there and take a look. After a day of clearing debris with shovels and picks, they had created an opening large enough for Posey and Kierstein to get through. When they squeezed in between the rocks into the dark mine, Posey found what he had been searching for over the past two years, sitting untouched behind an iron door – the Ghent Altarpiece. Kierstein wrote later, "Calm and beautiful, the altarpiece was, quite simply, there."

Walking on, Kierstein and Posey discovered Michelangelo's *Bruges Madonna*. Days later, they found *The Artist's Studio* and *The Astronomer* by Vermeer. A week later, George Stout arrived, bringing with him a summary of the mine's contents that he received from a Nazi turned Allied-collaborator. Thousands of pieces of art were there including 6,577 paintings, 122 tapestries, 954 prints, and 137 sculptures. There were nearly 300 cases that had never been inventoried, so the contents were unknown.

With Stout in command, the Allies got to work at evacuating the mine. When he first looked at the list, Stout thought it would probably take a year. He did not have a year. President Harry Truman had agreed that Altausee would be Soviet territory by July 1. That left them four days to evacuate the entire mine. MFAA officers Thomas Carr Howe Jr. and Lamont Moore, along with German art restorer Karl Sieber, went into the mine to prioritize what needed to come out first. Using sheepskin coats as protection as Stout did at the mine in Merkers, delicate pieces were wrapped and then placed in crates. The crates were put on trolleys called mine dogs, which made their way on tracks through the mine. Mine workers followed the mine dogs and then the mine dogs were pulled out of the mine by a small engine. From there, the crates were loaded onto trucks, driven down the mountain roads and transported to the MFAA collection point in Munich.

Fortunately, the July 1 deadline stretched out into August. During that time, the MFAA men worked 16-hour days, sometimes in the rain, to evacuate the mine. Stout got an infection when he scraped his knuckles along the hard salty walls. There was little food, not enough light, and few places to sleep. But they got it done. When Eisenhower gave his order that important works be returned immediately, the Ghent Altarpiece was the first one to go home. From Heilbronn, with Harry Ettlinger supervising, 73 cases of stained glass windows from a cathedral in Strasbourg, France were returned. Having never been opened, the crates were able to bypass the collection points and go straight to France. For Strasbourg, it was a sign that they were, indeed, free from Nazi reign and free from centuries of German rule.

Collection Points

The MFAA set up major collection points in Munich, Wiesbaden, and Offenbach. Recovered art was sent to these points where it was inventoried, repaired, and, if possible, returned to its owner. James Rorimer had somehow managed to convince General Patton that he needed the former Nazi headquarters in Munich more than the illustrious general needed it as headquarters for his Third Army. The art poured in to the collection points from the various mines, monasteries, or holes in the ground where it had been stored. Germans were interviewed, and they told of other storage locations. The MFAA added more men and women as it was able in order to handle the work load. In fact, most of the MFAA officers came on board after the fighting ended.

By early June 1945, the Seventh Army had discovered 175 Nazi art storage facilities just in its territory alone. Each piece of art had to be transported to a collection point. By July, the Munich collection point was full so Rorimer opened a second large facility in Wiesbaden. Kenneth Lindsay, who was not so thrilled with the Army but had heard about Rorimer, applied for a transfer from the Signal Corps to the MFAA that July and was assigned to Wiesbaden. He recalled later that it was a "nightmare" getting the 300-room collection point operational. It was a former state museum building before the war and the Luftwaffe headquarters during the war.

One of the major problems with the building was that the windows had been blown out. Somehow, the new Monuments Men needed to find 2,000 pieces of glass. Walter Farmer, an interior decorator from Cincinnati, helped himself to glass from a nearby U.S. Air Force base. It was without permission of the Air Force, but the MFAA was desperate to have some protection for the art that would soon be rolling in. They had only two weeks to clear debris, get electricity working, repair roofs, close off underground passages, and assemble a staff that could be trusted with the work that were going to do.

The first convoy of trucks arrived at Wiesbaden on August 20. Fifty-seven trucks were escorted by armed tanks, led by James Rorimer. Lindsay recalled that as he scrambled to get the trucks unloaded, Rorimer complimented him on his work, which he said was the first and only compliment he ever received in the Army. One of the first treasured pieces that was unloaded that day was a painted bust of the Egyptian Queen Nefertiti. The 3,000 year-old statuette had survived the war and the workers were thrilled to see it intact. Debates continue today between Egypt and Germany about where Nefertiti should be. The bust was at Wiesbaden until 1955, where it was given to the Egyptian Museum in Berlin. Germany is unwilling to give it up, saying it was obtained legally, and it is too fragile to move.

Many pieces had no claimants, though. Among those are Torah scrolls and other religious pieces that were taken from Jewish synagogues all across Europe. The Monuments Men were well aware of how they ended up in their facilities and that their owners would not be coming to claim them because they did not survive. Lindsay said that the presence of the religious items was "unnerving." The work continues today in trying to match up records to owners of Torah crowns and put the crowns in the hands of the right families.

The Offenbach facility also opened in July 1945 when it became apparent that more space would be needed. The five-story building served as a factory before it became a MFAA collection point for over three million printed materials. When Seymore Pomrenze arrived, he said that the building was packed with papers, letters, books, Torah scrolls, and various other documents. The six workers already assigned to the facility did not know where to begin. Pomrenze started by adding over 160 staff, then made a guide of all identifying stamps and marking that could identify material by country of origin. Then each country was assigned a room or rooms. National representatives were then allowed to claim their material. To the Netherlands went 329,000 items, including books taken from the University of Amsterdam, to the French went 328,000 items, the Soviets reclaimed 232,000 items, and Italy received 225,000 items. Pomrenze eventually sent unclaimed documents to libraries in New York and Europe, as well as New York's YIVO Institute for Jewish Research.

Conclusion

Several of the Monuments Men remained in Europe, long after the fighting ended, completing their mission of returning stolen art to its rightful owner. Many went on to become leaders in the art world. However, their work during World War II has ramifications that will last for centuries. For many of the European cities, the return of their outstanding cultural symbols was an important step toward restoring the identity that Hitler
tried to steal. For the entire world, it was the rightful reclamation of the best that artists have had to offer.

Even into the 21st century, the work to return stolen art and cultural treasures continues. In 2009, 46 countries signed an agreement to make more of an effort to return art stolen during the Holocaust. In March 2013, France's Ministry of Culture announced that the country was making a concerted effort to return 2,000 pieces of stolen art to the Jewish families that originally owned them. The internet offers an invaluable tool that previous museum directors and curators did not previously have, which makes researching art and family records infinitely more simple. As more stolen art resurfaces, the call has grown for museums to do the morally responsible thing and see that it is returned.

However, without the work of the Monuments Men – and women – none of what is happening today would be possible. Their diligence and dedication proved that saving a culture was not merely about saving lives and battling for territory, but preserving the art that makes life worth living. As Robert Edsel, the founder of the Monuments Men Foundation put it, "Their search was the greatest treasure hunt in history."

References

Adams, Paul. "U.S. Veteran Returns Art Album Taken from Hitler's Villa." BBC News. January 29, 2010.
http://news.bbc.co.uk/2/hi/americas/8486092.stm

Berge, Richard, et al, Directors. 2006. *The Rape of Europa.* (Documentary.) USA.

Edsel, Robert M. The Monuments Men. New York: Center Street. 2009.

Monuments Men Foundation.
http://www.monumentsmenfoundation.org/bio.php?id=296

Poole, Robert M. "Monumental Mission." *Smithsonian Magazine.* February 2008.
http://www.smithsonianmag.com/history-archaeology/monumental-mission.html?c=y&page=4

Printed in Great Britain
by Amazon